Suicide Psalms

Other books by Mari-Lou Rowley

CosmoSonnets, JackPine Press
Viral Suite, Anvil Press
Interference with the Hydrangea, Thistledown Press
Boreal Surreal, LyricalMyrical
CatoptRomancer, Relevations Publications
a Knife a Rope a Book, Underwhich Editions

Suicide Psalms

suicide psalms

POETRY BY

Mari-Lou Rowley

anvil
PRESS

Anvil Press Inc.
P.O. Box 3008, Main Post Office
Vancouver, B.C. V6B 3X5 canada
www.anvilpress.com

First Printing.

Library and Archives Canada Cataloguing in Publication

Rowley, Mari-Lou, 1953-
    Suicide psalms : poetry / by Mari-Lou Rowley.

ISBN 978-1-895636-92-5

    I. Title.
PS8585.O8957S93 2008   C811'.54   C2008-904691-9

Printed and bound in Canada
Cover design: Mutasis Creative
Interior design & typesetting: HeimatHouse

Represented in Canada by the Literary Press Group
Distributed by the University of Toronto Press

The publisher gratefully acknowledges the financial assistance of the Canada Council for the Arts, the Book Publishing Industry Development Program (BPIDP), the Saskatchewan Arts Board and the Province of British Columbia through the B.C. Arts Council and the Book Publishing Tax Credit.

In memory of my lost father

Vernon Placatko

1927 to 1953

A hole instead of arms to fall into.

Contents

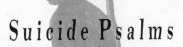

Suicide Psalms

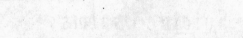

1

bridges, this city of sky
whoa, who jumps there?

shaking rails a train's approach
wood fatigue
metal fatigue
tired transoms
old garters and opacity

sorry speech neglect
neg lect
negative lecture
legislated nomenclature
of shotgun-spattered sand
birds feasting on bits of flesh

tell me about it
dis moi

pigeons in the girders
lying low, cooing

2

smell of melancholy
intended aphorism
on the cutting floor
kill sites bedded with violets

begotten and begotten
rancid sweet nostalgia
old woman's toilet
jars and jars

stacked
for winter, cold cellar
and alone, the wind fingers
all possible points of entry
conclusions, ways out

winter, white out, walking
out into the white night
so strong the wind
so soft the snow

3

stroboscopic, a rare bite
down like a brick
nova and nova she goes

the flag's flap gapping laugh
half down or half up
suspended, suspense

cuts the air like bullets
thinly, ballistic silvertip
from a 30-aught-six

the size of hole from that distance
better to shoot up
and to the left, sideways

glance at the moment of release
body mass lighter by twenty-one grams
soul juice discharge

of charged particles, all the better
to see you by, my dear, this
phosphorescent kiss

4

possible incursions into ionospheres
of guilt, please release us
let us go darkly
into that quiet night
remembering

a handsome handler
tongue and prick
backwash and augury

denial the fulsome weight of survival
funambulist who has always fumbled
with edges, clung
to the top of edifices

a plane goes by unnoticed

when you breathe in the air bubbles
lungs water tears
I want to go quietly you say
make no mistakes

afterward hawks circle overhead
their needy swoop of desire
pinioned against the bright sky
their skrees of delight

5

dimple squeak
fingering above coccyx
nightly emissions of remorse
rock a bye rock a bye

scalene limbo
neck stretch admissible
a knot is tied and untied
a guffaw somewhere

too dark to tell
the smell of canvas
too late to tell
you everything I know

or ever wanted

lace curtains flutter
in the breeze
a promise
take me

6

collaborative mapping
of syntax to sigh
beneath the white spruce
beneath foreign daggers
beneath the underbelly

a way through the morass
of taffeta and velvet high-
school promenade, devilishly
in hot pants, fishnet
in a sleeping bag

bugs, branches
fur and skin, tongue tricks
willow switch
quicksand and river's
thick sucking under

marine green algae
nostril gills
smell of sushi and mud
jackfish glint and wink
wait patiently

7

the telling is the telling is the telling
stay with me awhile
forget blessings
embrace neutral adornment
travel at the speed of night
eternally, a gift

a sigh is a sigh is a sigh
madam butterfly in the background
hovering beyond recognition
moth-wings weeping dust-sad tales
of love and regret

nostalgia nicotine-stained
on the walls, in the closet
cat hair, old socks, fur balls
his teeth in a jar

toaster ghosts whisper
conspiracies of fire
abundant ashes of morning
grim light
through half-dead trees

birds twitter for crumbs
life dependencies intertwined

in China plates of sparrows
feed visiting dignitaries
hummers and bumblers all

take my hand my love
exhale your sigh
your gone dream

8

for Tom Thomson

expert angler disgruntled by weather
wolverine dreams in the afternoon

deeper, into the thick bush
brushes singed
gold, russet, indigo

the canvas of forest and night

disappearance mysterious
the story goes

a canoe capsizes
a star goes nova
pulsars signal radio songs
over here over here

such a man does not
stand up in a boat
drop cigar ash
in the underbrush

9

fingering

finger puppets
pulpit   pupae
good
pupil
dilates to take
it all in
all   all
  in   in   in
deed
  in
word
  in
thought

ain't misbehaving

  again again

red stain
white socks
black patent shoes

knees pitted with gravel

gavel, worms
gargoyles and larvae coil
under gravestones

safe at last

10

bronchial colic cloisters dust
into ducts, tubes
air forced this way and that

lungs of the house lull into dream
wizards with limp wands
    old doodads
this persistent witch
doesn't need
paraphernalia

a remedy or two for cold and flu
plantain picked from alleys
kidney tonic or potent poultice
rub until moist, press
gently onto open wound
bind tight, leave for one day
and one night

cellular repair encoded in the body's thoughts

the wound should not fester
the scab should not scar
the ache should not remain
the heart should not open
again

II

diva of the Diaspora
weltering wail
sweltering sun
sand-knuckled
belt-buckled
zip-locked
shaved and taped
the weight of lead
against heart

hear the sea so near so near

bird tongues clicking tremolo
the whistle
of heavy artillery
in the middle of night
back against wall
face against stone
blood against bone

hear the sea so near so near

12

moon rakes against sky
throat rattle, wolf gaze
pupil pierced with night
dilation no longer viable

swagger a congestion of the hips
an excuse for everything
belittled litany a kind of joke
sliver under nail
blood blister
pickled eggs
sour carpet
pungent perfume

hip to hip
thumb to throat
rope to rafter
boot to stool

you picked a fine time to leave me
on the juke box

13

admire me
yellow daffodil dress
puffy skirt white
socks, underpants

bind her, behind
the shed in the yard
an old shovel
rust-stained
ochre-coloured
dried earth blood

nostril flame
filaments of sex somewhere
a stamen, somewhere
a pistol

14

arraignment adorned
or abandoned
on the highway
out of town

discarded loosely
a not-adored daughter

even now longing
counterfeits memory
conjures
booze cans, gambling joints
rancour-flattened faces
mean-mouthed cigar-smoking
deal-makers
soul-takers

take me with you
take me
with you

daddy

15

awl, cloak and dagger
behind the bed
skeletons rattle
bleak reeking bones

go away get away
neighbourhood nostradamus
wanker bugger fucker

tennis balls under blouse
for breasts
grasshoppers
under skirt
squirm and spit
tobacco juice
an old man's game
buzzard and spittle

another kid another mother
finger in face
don't you ever
dare go there

16

down under
water swirls to the left
flushed caplets twirl madly down
regurgitated Seconal
a second chance

under
the covers
under the bed
down under
there

down done dead
soul plunge
auger to hole
spud it spud her
spud her on down

finger plunger purge
and release
get it get it
get it all
out

17

caged bliss
an afterthought
of love
me tender
love me blue

and black
holes poked through
eye throat heart

open and tender
atrial rhythms
p-wave erratic
ectopic erotic

womanizer
tenderizer
sanitizer
pulverize
her

18

crash tested, burnt again
rampiked
spindly spruce
tear the sky to tears

old growth
knuckles fungied under
knee moss
heel on sternum

they went thataway
he said, waving the gun

blind sided, blind-eyed
world-weary
stars
turn their faces
holes everywhere

moribund leaking raging
floods, tempests, viruses

come on, mutate! replicate!
jump species jump
ship, let's get it
over with

19

pug-faced, thick-lipped
black padded Buick

black-suited men
in the back seat
with black guns
slick-backed hair

in the front seat
you beside the driver

at home mother and me
at her breast

but you beat them
to it
huh daddy?
hah!

20

fungal outcrop of dormant spores
grandpa loved mushrooms
memory of home, lilacs, pilsner
Kafka's black jokes
history wound up
in town clocks
Terrezine, bloody spring
memories lost somewhere

names misspelled
by officious officials
Placatko instead of Placatka
just another Polak
they scoffed

so I never knew
how to spell your name
how to find your grave
how to tell you anything

21

mood portal
tongue in groove
swerve control
the better to steer you by
my dear
rough terrain, hurricanes

swelling in the brain
encephalitic ensilage
fodder for future
fits and storms

another kind of weather mapping

serotonin gauge
hormonal readouts
neuronal firing
electrocardio impulses
fluid secretion rate
blood flow

serous intentions
heinous intervention

22

intravenous coiling
into and out of
hope, consciousness

guilt simmering
throat ache, heart kick
wretched and retching

to watch him go
not gently
not quietly
too young
too dark
too late

23

dead flesh feels
like refrigerated
chicken skin

when I go
I want my face
stretched smooth

blissful smiling lie
lying there
hands folded neatly
over unbroken heart

before the crackle
of fat burning
before the ashes

I want scattered
just so, my spot
along the river

not where I once
almost jumped

the sting of first love
biting back on itself
the way deception
alters colour, sound

the velvet black ribbon of river
a body bag, unzipping

24

bodily palimpsest
an unfettering
a way between or away
the constant nocturnal knock
behind the eyes

dreaming an eagle's
air-spread feathers
soaring on thermals
up mountain cliffs
the rush of the dive

off the overpass
drivers taken by surprise
by the jump
by your concrete awakening

body splayed, not
entirely broken
after the splints
electroshocks, hot baths
aftermaths

the voices you hear
not lingual, primal
utterance a murmur
fly, fly, fly!

dendrite spines adjudicate psychotropics
this one makes you larger
this one so small
you want to crawl down
into the pock-marked
ravenous night

eat me, devour all
flesh, organs, entrails
burn the bones or stack them
neatly to bleach in the sun
make a tower for ants
to traverse, at the top
leave some crumbs
in the hollow of scapula
scraped clean of burning
rhomboids deltoids

steroids opiates
barbiturates
sudafed tylenol
codeine caffeine
amphetamine cocaine
mescaline
rock and roll

alcohol
ortho novum
carcinoma
heart murmuring
out of sync fibrillation
first degree AV
blocked attempts
and after all
these years
still here

26

hushed deciduous dictum
whisper of poplar accusatory
branches too weak
for a rope, a body

a scene demanding answers –
farmhouse abandoned
lace curtains still billowing
over the broken window
canning pot on the cupboard
dusty coats on the rack
teddy bear
on cracked floorboards
rusted tractor, plough
root-bound

while poppies reseed themselves
in the once-abundant garden
plucked restlessly
by a woman
child-weary
too young
not ready
for life

wasp caught in a web
enraged wrangle and hiss
a twist, a coiling out
back to life

who was your spider
daddy?
my dandy dreamer
known only in dreams

the one who snared you
candy caner
cuttle shunter
tool handler
ring pawner
dream debaser

lure and lurch ·
the seductive snare
of dragline silk
trapped you cocoon-like
relinquished finally

no coiling out

28

beware
con elixirs
daughter debauchers
slouched in doorways
sleazy upstairs offices

perennial paramours of dissatisfaction
pariahs with blond hair
black moustaches
handlers who turn you over
for a buck

over and over
white skin
white sheets
white powder
white out

29

grazed again
   glazed over
gut and gall and bile

piebald parable of self
retractions definitive
burn traces and smoke
the smell of singed skin
defaced monuments

moments like that never die
she remembers the muscled padding
where his palm joined thumb

dances alone now

all right all right

father
conjurer
catapult dancer
gypsy diviner

your dream
a cabin a river a nest a gun
for shooting game
a rod for catching fish
an axe for chopping

wood, fallen along the path
rampiked and cinder dry

ethereal whisperer
infant bawl
crow caw
me unexpectedly

all those receding rivers
calling you out
into the fallen night

bequeathing
your smell
your whisper
your tall shadow
lost dreams

31

limb-trammelled
stumbling toward the drove

love hammers all
feigning

tinder among the crowds
panic builds in the dugout

a curveball to the heart
pop of wood against skull

bleeding along the baseline
a negated re-entry

who knew who would succumb
tombolas of longing

32

shush there! no need
for chain rattle, door slam
moving the statue
face against wall
to hide her
mahogany breasts
heavy and pointed away

why take that glass
from the top cupboard
make that sound
wake me

lie down now
rest peacefully
forget betrayals
the gun to the head
your public outpouring

je comprends
JÁ dovídat se
I understand

no longer wanting
to be

33

keen shuttle
back and back again

road enclosure
a broad brush to
wash you out with
stroke after stroke

picaresque
the shrill hee hee
white-throated
sparrow laugh

underbrush erasure
ants and flies
ravens and crows
carrion cleaners

gaze into the swirl of ferns
spiral down into thick brush
sink down into soft moss
dissolve to black

discandied

atom by atom
quark by quark
flavour by flavour

34

coming unhinged
dossiers of self
dissolve in the aftermath
a way of once being
together
gone

that walk that path those leaves
differently

body all
chilled particles
no electrons jump
to higher states
no transfer of heat
no energy

hollowed veins drain
in blue-lipped grimace
dilated stare of once-amber eyes

you've gone and done it now
damn it
gone
damn you

35

non-neutral annihilation
industrial therapy
playing in the red zone

stop not an option

slit slacker hacking forth
gangling
a slow burn
electric fence
cigarette
gas oven
unwatched candle

got a light
get lit
the burning bubbling spoon
dealers in dockyards
old track lines
on the arm
hanging from the dumpster
a trace of finger nail
in the pigsty

gun-metal eyes
gun-metal sky

36

survival preparation
sentiment force-fed
all those old tunes
eat enough for ten
and then some

medicated hibernation
manipulated seed
animals bred with straws of sperm
no body contact
no kicking and braying

sterilized, injected, pumped
rage and mutation rampant

ah the smell
of Roundup in the morning

don't sit on the grass
don't eat the fruit
don't

37

heart hollow, hypertrophic
a dilation of longing
dream paths that go on and on
didactic distances
take this corner, up these stairs
a woman in a washroom
a chef with a cleaver
run running
leg ache intensified
with each leaden step
erratic heartbeat

the panic of the chase
of being so lost
so late
so empty

substance less
intransient trespasser
interloper in life
incapable of coherence
drifting fractals of self
spiral out and away

38

phantom in the distance
frustum materializing
from between a groyne of timber
frames of bony spires

their falling an embraceable erasure
without
reference points
landscape
horizons

I want you to know I know this

so busy looking for gold
you missed the ground
froth flotation a methodology
for mineral exploitation
bubbles adhere only to ore
float it on up
leaving solid earth

others would see black soil, nourishment
you, gangue and ash

39

neuropathic ever since
gone a long while
the nebulous leverage
of leave-taking
slinking off silently
remorse inversely incremental
to relief

he remembers the mole
soft brown nevus a cluster
of vessels on her shoulder

her body a vessel
to lose oneself in
her seas deep, turbulent
swells and storms

inhaling incidental in the
whirlpool vertigo
eyes closed, mouth open
a drowning thing she laughs

he laughs over beer
with the boys
eyes closed, mouth open
a long swallow
another
and another
whirling vertigo
nightly drowning

40

potentate promise
kiss this cross
this ring
hail these marys
suck this dick
wassail and nails
thorn-grooved
skull and buckets of brine
a cup floweth

over the top
she dances away godma
topless in the woods
girlish gaia
turned guilt goddess
turned
table dancer
lap dancer
chicken dancer

ghost dancer

41

gorge reward
anon anon
the horizon just over there
there
the lip the edge
the ledger
rolled in throes of thunder
names called anonymously

you for dithering madly
you for blame and curse
you for nothing
nil nada

echo exit, tensile
taut
scalene sinew
jugular sheaths

disappointment
a hard line
a dull knife
an unsteady hand

42

saddled, blighted
stones thrown into trees, face

decrees of slate chipped from
boulder-disfigured shoulders

your grieving blaming
smothering

mother love/load
lost to him/me

for a time
for a time

43

tracking the wide portal
moongrass shuttle
eyes closed tight behind fists
a kaleidoscope of greens, blues
purple

imagine a night without fear
or imagining

fabled escape
hatched under blankets
flashlight subterfuge
throttle and throttling

he sets his father's favourite hammer
on a little raft
floats it downstream
a small boy's wonder
minced with hatred

sculptural
palpable

44

anglers indulging
phosphorus bliss rends out
bottom-feeders
from dank mud
the reek of methane
algae overkill

understandably in the afternoon
ontological
a bonding event
father, son
barbed hook catches lip ring
slice and screech

ravens such angry birds
forest goths
killjoys
nihilists

you owe me you sonofabitch

a day in the sun
dangerous history

45

hooked
hook her up
barbed, baited
breather
thumb under gills
aftershock of air
bad fish analogy
biting madly

nails hair muscular tissue
swollen fossa
anatomical pit or groove
evidence of forced exit
out and out
a throw back
too small ugly dumb

don't talk about
group gropes
crotch grab tit squeeze
    her in a corner
fish breath! slime smell!
don't tell or we'll
kill you really
we will

46

greying rectitude of sky
instances forgotten
a wearying of words
of worlds

bag flap
door jamb
bedevilling and idle
time and time
again
meaning diminished

edgewise rustle of insects in grass
amplification of the diminutive
humble harbingers
menial things
a stone with a bud of granite
dragonflies' glorious turquoise
    head to tail coupling
a swallow chasing a raven
    from its nest
a kill site's slow decomposition

life simply
going on

Hermitage Poems

Day One

White out.

Electrostatic
sky   snow   seamless
under sky so wide
over ground so deeply buried.

Above claws of trees
a flock of birds flits and darts
     gust-skidding
shrill peeps of delight
in free-fall, frivolous flight.

Day Two

Snow silence
                    drifting
thoughts crystalline
Burtonesque
vibraphone chill
no birds chirp
dogs bark
engines roar,
only the wind's
thin throat song
            train memory.

Day Three

Inside
frigid wind-breath
etches forests of frost
between frame, window.

Outside
dead twigs poke holes in snow,
sparrows huddle
all sepia and beige.

Nostalgia is not as simple as this.

Across the field
a lone man lumbers
then disappears
behind a line of trees
or under a drift of snow.

Day Four

crusty cornice of drift
a cliff for leaping snow spiders

edges of wind slice jaw
nape of neck, wrist

a deer leaps into the woods
hoof tracks on snowshoe trail

along the cemetery hedge
woodpeckers at eye level

black Zorro masks
with bright crimson patches

Day Five

Sun dog biting day
eerie haloed omen
fractured rainbow, finger
of refracted light
poking into the snow-deep field
signalling change
in the fluid flow
of weather.

Minus 30 and blowing

not colder I pray, dreading
the frigid trek back
to warmth, food,
thinking like the deer
must think.

Day Six

Sunstreams illuminate motes of dust,
the coral aura behind eyelids
heavy, heavier.

Mantra of freight train's
thunder and click
steel-wheeled melancholy
of a country song.

Snow melts on the bird bath
jets crisscross the sky,
pilots g-force grinning
as they search for glory,
patrol for terrorists.

Day Seven

Sun licks twisted bark,
melting primordial knots
on bony shoulders.

Sudden hollow snap overhead
more like tongue click –
thogngnk to the left,
thogngnk thogngnk
to the right,
woods alive with tongue clicks of trees
   stretching limbs
       thawing muscles
heralding warmer weather.

Day Eight

Toward the dark wood
sentinel spruce converge
in one-point perspective
at the cemetery gate.

Gnarled twigs brush
against face, hands
of voiceless ghosts
gesture sad tales, tug
like a small child's cry
hear me, hear me.

At last, the clearing
dull moon metal sky
Orion's sword
gleaming alpha male promise
you're safe under me baby.

Day Nine

Wind again.

Sky hazed with sun shrapnel
no comfort in its light,
        all moisture
sucked from eyes, nose
fingers cracked raw.

Finally the cabin.

Door frozen shut,
knob stuck tight
as an oyster shell
memories of the sea flooding.

Eyes to keyhole
hot breath to lock
shoulder to wood
boot to frame
will to resistance.

The door opens
to warmth, and the click
of heater kicking in
hot tea with sugar milk apple cream cheese
Spanish olives.

Day Ten

God's Dog Boy

Face pressed into straw
he tries to picture
coyotes playing and fucking in the field,
frail wrists flat out, dog paws,
ass pulled up in the air.

Jesu christi, in nomini patri
wag your tail for him
ecum spirit TU TU OH
the young pups squeal high on the wind.

Pater noster pray for me,
this hour of darkness
smells of carcases, shit, chickens.

Dog boy, coyote boy, get up off your knees,
think of Jesus, jeezus, JEEZUS!
the big man groans,
throws and mounts him
again again   again.

The boy howls like coyotes in the field
dog paws flat out, bum in the air
hair caked with dirt and scum.

When he wakes up the coyote
is licking his ass, his face, uncurling
the tight fist of his body.
Then God's dog saunters off,
kills a chicken or two.

Day Eleven

Today clouds obscure sun again
a day of negative space.

The sound of laughter intrudes
I want only lull,
no conversation.

Freight train's whine stirs longing
to be gone   somewhere.

Pills dropped into daily slots —
50 mg. of Flecainide
keeps heart in rhythm,
no wild racing, no skipping,
no atrial fibbing,
no fun at all.
10 mg. of Tamoxifen
keeps cancer in check.
20 mg. of Celexa
holds black dogs at bay.

The body out of balance a
pitiful thing.

The world out of balance
the black dog's joke.

Day Twelve

hush
snow-muted
swing in the body
      its sticky weight.

dappled grey falling sky
cold prick
of clustered flakes
belie an underbelly
of acid
the choking stratosphere.

sparrows huddle in bush, chirping
waiting it out
      cheerfully.

Day Thirteen

Owl Syntax

Nightwalk back under moon's crescent grin
creak of boots on snow hardened by wind.
Imperfect rhyme, rhythm of iambic step
interrupted by an owl's call
Oowh hooo, Hoo oowh Hoo.

I answer — Hoo, Hoo, woow Hoo,
wondering if the lost syllable
means anything personal, unsure
of owl vocabulary, syntax.

Ooowh, Whoo Hoo
he calls back three plaintive syllables.
I answer, too ardently perhaps
yet it goes on like this all down the path,
around the corner, through the trees,
call and response, two creatures speaking
our yearning across species,
the language
of night and sound.

Day Fourteen

Snow Sirens   *for Anne Szumigalski*

Gaze-dazzled
snow showing off
a spectroscopic dance
    blue green red
frequencies so clear and pure
you want to remember
only this.

Waist-high drifts   beckon
for the crush of crystals under hushed footsteps
on windblown spines.

Let us throw our snowy limbs around you
here, lie down with me
my angel
spread your arms/legs
wide to the sky   feel
the gentle tug of earth,
the caress and release of sinking.

       Close your eyes.
Feel your breath crystallize and rise
one last time.

Survival Psalms

That when you are here
I am here   fully
awake, wide, ready
and beyond wanting
you to uncurl me.

That again the well of footprint
high-arched and light
in the gleaming silica,
waves, squalls
white gulls and children
playing.

That no more tankers,
missiles, settlements —
a beach for all
that is best in us
to well up and wade in
a play of worlds.

That tomorrow and tomorrow
and tomorrow
a beginning again
    always
species survival even in
tempests, disaster, chaos,
greed-mutated genes.

That I want, whenever I see you,
a world of thanks
emblazoned on the pen
I write with.

That the meek don't give in
the poor don't give up
the rich don't want
to get any richer.

That always reindeer lichen
and sand heather,
fern and dewberry
compatible codominants
of the understory.

That trees burn or fall
when they are ready.

That we learn when enough is enough
and how not to fear death.

That something better rises out of the ashes.

That aurora permeable in the moment
raven wing, poplar rustle,
dry binding whine of wind
        wrap me   wrap me
stories enfolded in foliage
encrusted in calcite
all the miners' bones, crunched
        into tailings,
newfound carbon sinks
that speak of loss and gain,
despair and hope,
a new way of looking.

That more and more
want less and less.

That food, water, love
are not wasted.

That a sky so clear
all stars in Orion's sword
all seven sisters of the Pleiades
all moons and suns and planets.

That statesmen [not paladins
not palaverers] keep promises
and palms free
from grease and oil-
backed inveigling.

That beauty honour truth
become fashionable again.

That throat songs of
loons, grouse, cranes, sparrows,
all winged and flying things
open and heard clearly
joyously and always
soaring.

That inevitable is not the same
as destructible.

That unfolding fully
wide, ready awake
        unabashed
the moment in which
you are away not here
I want open and loudly
your hand cupping,
mouth uncurling.

That we altogether
somehow survive.

Acknowledgements

My appreciation and thanks to the Saskatchewan Arts Board and the Canada Council for financial assistance, and to the Saskatchewan Writers Guild Writers/Artists Colonies for the space and time to write this book. And to *Rampike, Rhubarb Magazine, Grain* and *subTerrain* for publishing some of these poems.

Love and thanks to Di Brandt for her ongoing support and enthusiasm, and for challenging me to follow the coyote. To Paul Dutton for his perpetual friendship, keen ear and wise editorial observations. To David Lee for his astute comments and writerly support. Love to Albert Lowe for being with and beside me. Love and thanks to Rhona McAdam, Kathleen Whelan, Sylvia Legris, Jennifer Still, Steven Smith, Hilary Clark, Robert McNealy, Barbara Klar, Beatriz Hausner, Betsy Rosenwald, Mary Walters, Holly Luhning, Elyse St. George, Nancy Senior, and Alice Kuipers for providing creative input, support and encouragement. Thanks to the monks at St. Peter's Abbey for sharing their home. My deep gratitude to Barry Segal and David Rugg. And to all those who have been important in shaping my work over the years: Christopher Dewdney, for inspiring me to tackle science; Anne Szumigalski, for challenging me to trust my instincts; Fred Wah, for helping me to find the voice between; Don McKay, for making me realize that I am a nature poet after all. To those I have forgotten to mention, thank you.